Secrets To Trading Candlestick Patterns:

Discover the Three Secrets to Profitable Trading with Candlestick Patterns.

James K. Roush

Table of Contents

Disclaimer

Forex trading, Stocks, or other financial instruments involves a high level of risk and is not appropriate for all investors. Past performance is not indicative of future outcomes. The high degree of leverage is risky and can work against you as well as for you. Before opting to invest in foreign exchange you should carefully assess your investment objectives, the level of experience, and risk tolerance. It is quite probable that you will experience a loss of part or all of your original investment and so you should not invest money that you cannot afford to lose. Do your own study and speak to a competent financial planner in order to be aware of all the risks connected with foreign exchange trading, and get advice from an independent financial adviser before risking any funds.

All information provided herein is for educational purposes only and should not be taken as advice on how to invest the funds you have. Always talk with a professional financial planner or adviser before making any investment choices. I shall not be held accountable for any losses that arise in your account. You and you alone are responsible for deciding if you are comfortable accepting the risk in Forex trading.

Introduction

Are you a trader who wants to improve your trading strategies and become more profitable? If so, this book is for you. In this book "Secrets To Trading Candlestick Patterns," you will learn three powerful techniques that can turn your trading around. By combining candlestick patterns like the hammer candle, engulfing candle, and shooting star candle with confluence from major structure levels, RSI overbought/oversold, and EMA 50, you can gain an edge in the market. This book will teach you how to spot the candlestick patterns, and how to form strategies to trade. You will also learn how to identify the best candlestick patterns and with this knowledge, you can become a profitable trader. The book will also provide you with trading rules and trade examples that use the best candlestick patterns mentioned in this guide. So, in this book, I'm going to share these three secrets and strategies with you and show you how you can apply them to your own trading so that you can become a master of candlestick pattern trading yourself.

Chapter one

Secret number one

So secret number one is divided into two parts.

Part one is Trading Candlestick Pattern with the trend and against the trend

So, let's move on to the first part. Now, when we're trading candlestick patterns, it's important to know what to look for. I want to explain what we're actually looking for. A lot of trading instructors will draw out a trend like this.

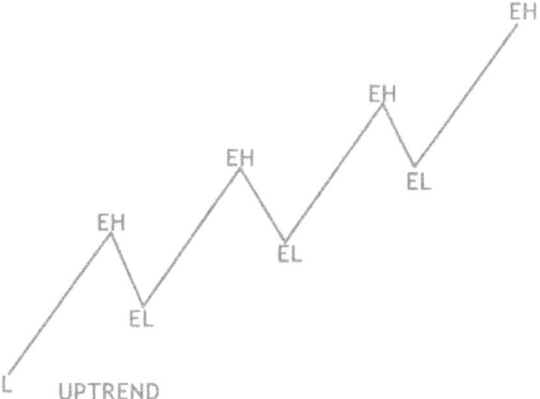

UPTREND

Yes, that indeed represents an uptrend, but it's not something that we encounter frequently in real-life trading scenarios. In reality, the price movement usually looks more like this:

We have price moving upwards, followed by a period of consolidation, and possibly another impulsive move. Eventually, the price continues to rise higher and higher. When we're trading candlestick patterns in a trending market, we need to focus on two things - **Extreme Highs (EH) and Extreme Lows (EL),** also known as **Major Swing Highs and Major Swing Lows.** It doesn't matter what you call them, but let me point them out for you in a counter trend perspective.

Counter Trend Perspective

When it comes to trading, going against the trend can be a high-risk but potentially high-reward strategy. It requires a good understanding of market dynamics and the ability to identify opportunities that others may overlook.

Personally, I have found this approach to be effective, but it is crucial to execute it correctly. One of the key considerations when using a counter-trend strategy is to identify the right entry point. In this case, we are looking for extreme highs in an uptrend, which can serve as a potential reversal point. Once we have identified the extreme high, the next step is to look for a suitable candlestick pattern at that extreme high.

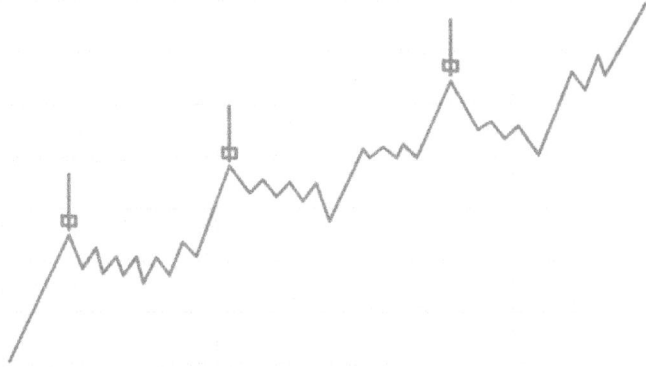

So when the price is moving upwards and breaking into new highs, it's important to look for a specific candlestick pattern at the top of that new high before placing a trade. This strategy gives us the best chance to capture a potential pullback and make a profit. To execute this strategy, we place trades at the very top of the trend, with a stop loss placed just above it. This ensures that if the price continues to rise, we get stopped out with minimal losses. Our target is set to achieve a favorable reward to risk ratio, which means we're looking for an opportunity to profit from the pullback that is likely to occur after the new high is reached. We repeat this process over and over again when we are counter-trend trading using candlestick patterns, maximizing our chances of winning trades.

Trend Continuation Perspective

Now on the trend continuation side of an uptrend, we'd be looking for the bottom of the pullback and we'd be looking for possible candlestick patterns at the bottom of the pullback in order to capture the next impulsive move higher in an uptrend.

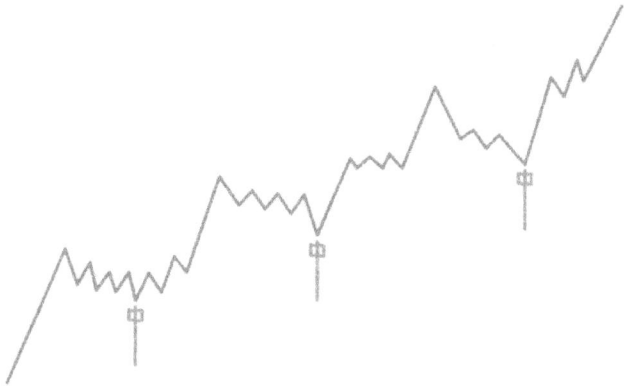

When we're dealing with an uptrend, it's important to keep an eye out for trend continuation opportunities. This means we should be looking for the bottom of the pullback, which can be identified by a swing low, and then seek out potential candlestick patterns at this point in order to capture the next impulsive move higher.

To illustrate this, let's take a look at an example of what it would look like in a downtrend. In a downtrend, we would see prices gradually declining over time. In this scenario, we would be interested in capturing the very bottom of the trend in order to profit from the potential pullback.

By identifying the major swing low in the downtrend, which is the very bottom of the trend, we can position ourselves to take advantage of the reversal. This would involve looking for counter trend trades that allow us to capture some profit on the pullback, all these new lows would be considered the major swing low in this downtrend.

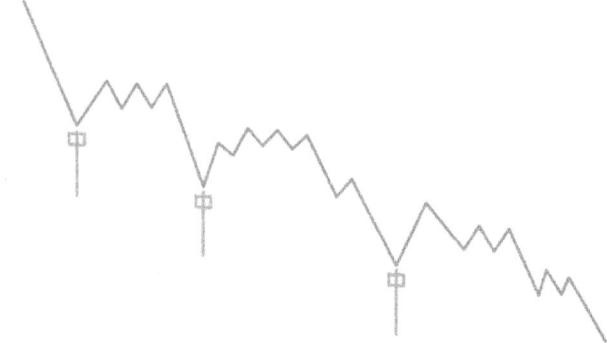

Next up for trend continuation, we're trying to capture the very top of a pullback with a candlestick pattern in order to capture the next impulsive move down that breaks below our structure level.

So we're looking for the tops of these pullbacks to give us a candlestick pattern. However, it's important to keep in mind that no strategy is 100% and there may be instances of fakeouts in both trend continuation and counter trend trading. But this is what we're trying to do with candlestick patterns.

Part number two of secret number one is having rules for your candlestick pattern.

It's crucial to have precise rules for identifying the specific candlestick pattern you're trading, whether it's hammers, shooting stars, or engulfing patterns. This eliminates any second-guessing and ensures that you're executing your trades based on a clear and well-defined strategy.

We will primarily focus on hammer and shooting star candles, and I would like to share my set of rules for identifying these patterns with you. These rules have been developed through extensive research and analysis, and are set in stone to provide clarity and consistency for identifying hammer and shooting star candles.

So let's take a closer look at the hammer and shooting star candlestick patterns and the specific rules for identifying them..

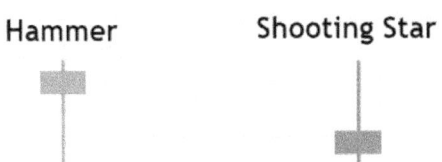

Hammer   Shooting Star

You can see a hammer and a shooting star candle. And the way I define these, in order to keep myself consistent and never second guess whether I'm actually seeing a hammer or a shooting star candle is by utilizing a Fibonacci retracement tool.

- ***For a Hammer candle:*** When looking for a Hammer candle, I use the Fibonacci retracement tool from the low of the candlestick up to the high of the candlestick. If the entire body of the candlestick is above the 38.2% retracement (indicated by the red line), then I consider it a valid hammer candle. The opposite is true for a shooting star candle.

Hammer

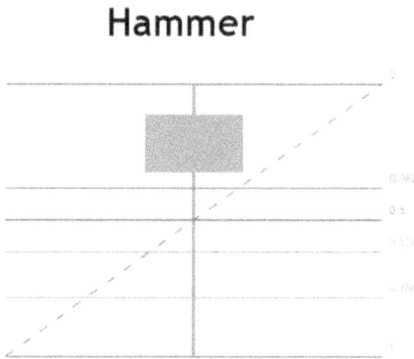

- **For a shooting star candle:** When identifying a shooting star candle, I look at the candle from its high point down to its low point. If the entire body of the candle is situated below the 38.2% retracement, I consider it as a shooting star candle.

Shooting Star

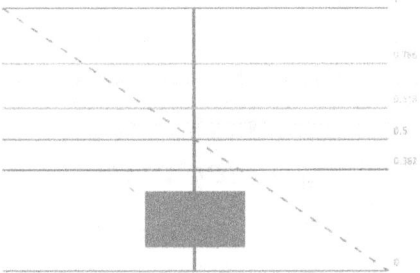

So hopefully that gives you some more clarity on what I mean by having set in stone rules for the candlestick pattern you're using. That way you can stay consistent and you're never second guessing whether or not the candlestick pattern you're trying to use is actually there on the chart.

Chapter Two

Secret number two is never trade candlestick patterns without at least two other major technical confluences.

Now below is my list of major technical confluences that I use in combination with candlesticks.

My Confluence List

- Major Structure Level (MSL). Higher time frame is even better
- RSI Overbought or Oversold (OB/OS). Divergence is even better
- EMA Cross or Bounce. Both are even better.

To explain things a little bit more, let me give you a brief explanation. We previously discussed searching for potential counter-trend trades at the peak of the move, which occurs during an uptrend, right? We were referring to those levels that are marked with circles.

Well, if you're doing this in the middle of nowhere with no other confluences, then it's not a profitable way to trade. The only thing that makes candlestick patterns at major swing highs profitable is adding other confluences. Personally, I consider major structure levels as a good confluence. In fact, a higher time frame major structure level would be even better. What I normally count as a major structure level is a level that's either been tested multiple times or a level that sticks out like a sword thorn.

So in this case, this would be a major structure level that would help me make the decision to place this trade.

One of the primary confluence indicators that I utilize in my trading strategy is the RSI indicator. Specifically, I look for instances where the RSI indicator is overbought or oversold, and a divergence occurs. For instance, if prices are trending higher, but the RSI indicator is trending lower instead of higher as prices make higher highs, it creates a divergence. This would signal an opportunity for me to trade a candlestick pattern at a major structure level. However, I only trade candlestick patterns when I have two other major technical indicators in confluence.

Another key indicator that I utilize is the cross or bounce of an EMA. For this purpose, I prefer using the 50 EMA indicator. To enter a trade, I need to see price cross the EMA, followed by a pullback to the 50 EMA level to look for some type of candlestick pattern. This provides an opportunity to follow the trend to the downside, once the reversal of crossing the EMA occurs, or at least a possible reversal

To provide a better understanding, let's examine a few examples. By analyzing these trades, we can see that they would have been profitable if executed in real-time. Furthermore, the analysis behind these trades aligns precisely with what I have been teaching throughout this book. I utilized the same techniques that you are currently learning to enter into these trades. So, what exactly are we looking for? As we previously discussed, we want to see the lows in a downtrend create some type of candlestick pattern.

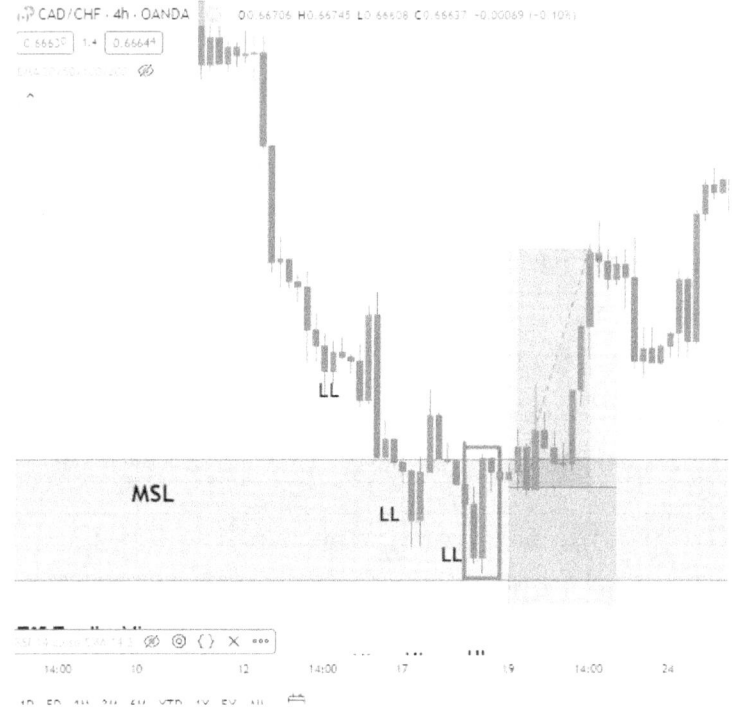

But that's not all we look for, because if that's all you look for, you will not be right more than you're wrong. You won't have a profitable strategy. We need to add some confluence to it. So the confluence I used on this specific trade consisted of two parts. Firstly, we do in fact have a major level of structure that sticks out like a sword thorn here on this example

and also outside of that major level of structure. If we pull up our RSI indicator, you'll see that we do in fact have RSI divergence as prices are making lower lows here. The RSI has started to make higher lows.

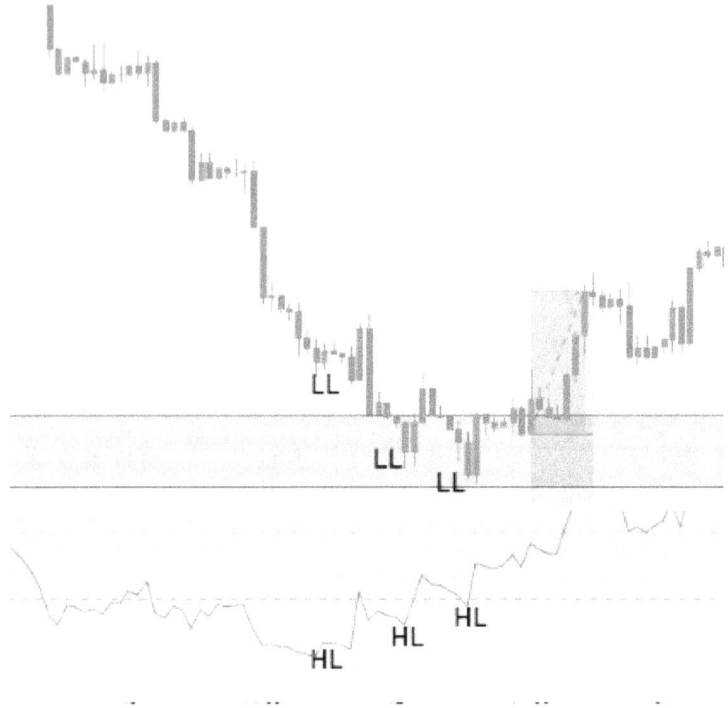

With that being the case, this is a great
example of RSI divergence combined with a
major structure level. And then this specific
trade was not utilizing a hammer candle, but
it did in fact utilize a bullish engulfing bar
right here.

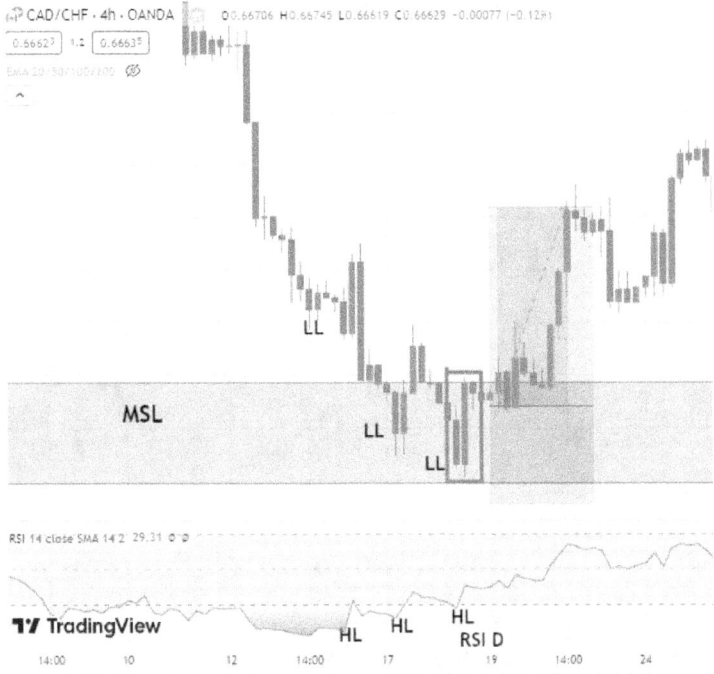

And that's when we got involved in this trade directly after that bullish engulfing bar. Hopefully that gives you a little more clarity of this situation.

Next is a bearish trade example on the pound dollar, utilizing the other confluences that we've already discussed. Let's take a look at that trade.

Based on what you've learned in this book,
can you identify the confluence I used on
this trade and the entry pattern? I hope you
were able to spot the entry pattern as it
meets the rules for a shooting star candle for
the way I trade them. The entire body of the
candle is below the 38.2% retracement.
Also, what is the confluence that we have?
We have the cross of the 50 EMA which is
my black line in the example below.
Although we didn't quite come up and touch

it, I count this as a bounce off the 50 EMA because of how close we got. We have a cross and a bounce off the 50 EMA, and with both of those occurring, I count that as two major technical factors.

After making the decision, I chose to go short when the shooting star candle closed. Therefore, as a conclusion to secret number two, I suggest that you should never solely rely on a candlestick pattern while trading. Instead, you must have at least two other significant technical factors aligned with that pattern. Again, These are the confluences that I personally prefer to use while trading.

My Confluence List

- Major Structure Level (MSL). Higher time frame is even better
- RSI Overbought or Oversold (OB/OS). Divergence is even better
- EMA Cross or Bounce. Both are even better
- Existing Chart Patterns (Head and Shoulders or Double Bottom/Double Top)

If you'd like to note them down and use them yourself, go ahead and do so.

Chapter Three

Secret number three is Existing Chart Patterns technique.

Most recently, I've been trading for a while now, and over the last couple of years, I've developed an advanced trading strategy that involves combining candlestick patterns with existing chart patterns. This approach has quickly become my favorite way to trade. By adding candlestick patterns to head and shoulders, inverted head and shoulder patterns, double tops, and double bottoms, I've been able to spot trends and make more informed decisions when placing trades.

Let me walk you through an example of a bullish trade where I would apply this strategy. Consider the dollar Swiss chart where the price is coming down. To most traders, a double bottom pattern is an opportunity to place a trade. However, there are two different ways to approach this pattern. One way is to wait for the first bottom to form, then the second one, and then enter the trade aggressively. This method works, but it doesn't always guarantee success.

With my approach, I wait for the first bottom to form and then look for a bullish candlestick pattern to confirm the trend. Once I spot the pattern, I wait for the price to retrace to the second bottom, and if it confirms the bullish pattern, I enter the trade using either bullish engulfing or hammer candlestick. This approach has proven to be more effective, and I've seen increased success rates.

So if you're tired of conventional trading methods and want to take your trading game to the next level, try combining candlestick patterns with existing chart patterns. It may take some time to master, but the rewards are worth it. So, let's take a look at the example below

When you see price push a bit higher after that second bottom, that would be a more aggressive way to trade a double bottom. A

more conservative trader may decide to wait for the break of the neckline of this double bottom.

That would be a more conservative approach to trading this double bottom. Trading a double bottom can be approached in different ways. One conservative approach is to simply wait for the double bottom pattern to form and then enter a trade. However, by incorporating candlestick patterns, it is possible to adopt a more moderate approach that is not as aggressive as waiting for the double bottom pattern to fully form, but also not as conservative as simply waiting for it to form. Here's what I mean: when using candlestick patterns in conjunction with existing chart patterns like double bottoms, we wait for the double bottom to form and then look for a specific candlestick pattern at the end of it. In this case, we're interested in the bullish engulfing pattern, which signals a potential upward trend. This specifically is an engulfing pattern.

So right here we have a valid double bottom which is then followed by a candlestick pattern being this engulfing pattern. So the exact way I personally trade using this type of setup is for me to wait for certain conditions to be met that is waiting for a scenario that meets my list of confluences.

To take a trade, I require at least two confluences. In this case, we already have the double bottom, which satisfies one of them. Another way to trade this is by pairing the existing chart pattern with a major level of structure, and then waiting for the candlestick pattern we want to see before pressing the buy button. Alternatively, I might use the RSI divergence method, which is what we're using in this trade scenario.

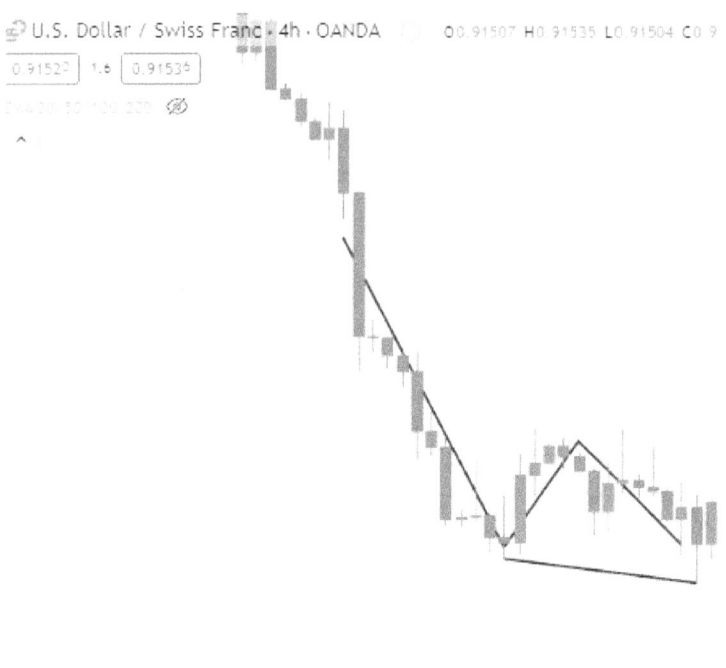

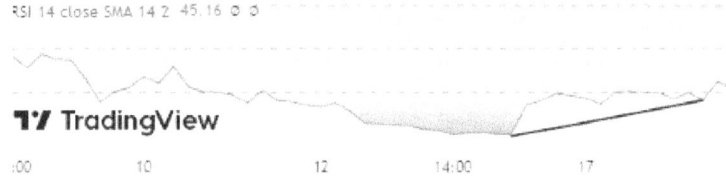

So if we look down at the RSI indicator, you can see we have a low right there, which is a low in price, we then get what? we get a lower low in price while the RSI indicator is making higher lows. So that is what we call

RSI divergence. So in this case, we have an existing chart pattern combined with RSI oversold divergence, and we have our candlestick pattern. Combining RSI oversold divergence with an existing chart pattern and candlestick pattern is my favorite way of trading candlestick patterns. So in this case, the way I would set up this trade would be something like an entry on the close of that engulfing candle or whatever candlestick pattern you choose to use, then a stop loss below the double bottom. The target would be, for me, my preferred reward risk ratio is between 1.4 and a 2.1, and for this trade, let's go with 1.4. While this trade happens to win, it's important to remember that every trade does not win.

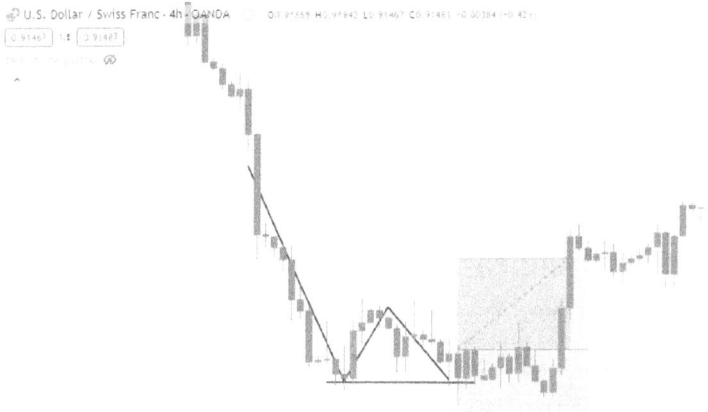

In order to give you a complete understanding of it, let's take a look at a bearish example. Hopefully this one is pretty easy for you to spot. But here we have a head and shoulders pattern followed by a candlestick pattern.

Let's see if you can point that out while I draw it for you. We have a push higher, followed by the shoulder of the head and shoulders pattern, followed by the neckline, the head of the head and shoulders pattern, and then the other part of the neckline. And what we have pushing up here at the second shoulder is a nice shooting star candle. Right here would be that shooting star candle.

So for this specific pattern, what I'm looking for is this head and shoulders. And at the end of the head and shoulders pattern, I want to see a candlestick pattern. A candlestick pattern like this shooting star candle. The trade setup would look something like this with an entry at the close of that candle, a stop loss just above it. And again, about a 1.4 to 1 reward to risk ratio is what I personally like to aim for with these trades.

As much as we'd like every trade to be profitable, it's not always the case. Nonetheless, it's worth noting that this particular trade ended up being favorable for us.

Conclusion

So understanding candlestick patterns in these three techniques of how to trade them and applying them will improve your trading. But trading comes down to a lot more than just understanding candlestick patterns. Now what I want to do is to let you know about trading expectations. A lot of new traders come into the market expecting to win every trade, but as I've said throughout this entire book, winning every trade is not possible. What we do as traders is we create a strategy using things like candlestick patterns and other technical confluence, and then we place trades based on that strategy over and over because it gives us an edge over a large sample size of trades.

The strategies that we've talked about in this book may win between 55 and 65% of the time. Now, when you think about that, it may sound good if you can get above a 1 to 1 and get above a 50% chance to win, that would be profitable over a long period of time. But what you're not thinking about is that out of every 100 trades, you will likely lose 40 to 45. You will lose nearly half of those trades, more than likely because no strategy is going to give you that 90% win rate with a 3 to 1 reward to risk ratio that I know I was looking for at the beginning of my trading career. And it took me a really long time to realize that that does not exist and that what we're doing again, as traders is creating a strategy and then letting the edge we have with that strategy with our combination of technical factors, we're letting that edge play out over a long period of time, and that will undoubtedly creates profitable trading. And if we do that consistently that way we can really build a trading account to massive size.

So as I end the book here, I'll advise you that you should go and study to help improve your trading skills. So, after learning about candlesticks, learning strategies, applying those strategies, creating your own strategy, whatever that may be after you have that strategy, there are other things you need to work on. You need to go study up on risk management. I don't care how you do it but you really need to learn about risk management and the effect it has on your emotions so that you can apply a good risk management plan while you're trading and also go study up on trading psychology to help you develop a disciplined trading mindset, which is necessary in achieving long-term success in trading.